Space Craft

Space Craft

Rich Murphy

RESOURCE *Publications* · Eugene, Oregon

SPACECRAFT

Resource Publications
An Imprint of Wipf and Stock Publishers
199 W. 8th Ave., Suite 3
Eugene, OR 97401

www.wipfandstock.com

PAPERBACK ISBN: 978-1-6667-0610-9
HARDCOVER ISBN: 978-1-6667-0611-6
EBOOK ISBN: 978-1-6667-0612-3

JUNE 28, 2021

For my children: Jacqueline, Matthew, Timothy, and Elizabeth

Contents

Stratosphere

Mesosphere

Thermosphere

Acknowledgments

"All Systems Go on the Potter Wheel," "Climate Climax," "20/20 Vision," and "Western Hemisphere Adult Education:" *Fractured Ecologies* (anthology);

"Practice Makes," "Under Lucky Stars," "Cultivate One's Own Garden:" *Terror House Magazine;*

"Zip:" *Leveler;*

"Space Cadet," *Former People;*

"Backseat Drivers" and "Bank Vault:" *BlazeVox;*

"Launch Pad" and "Cry from a Planet:" *New Texas;*

"The Human Refreshment:" *Sein und Werden;*

"Tai Chi to the Promised Land" and "Knowledge to Bear:" *Flatbush Review;*

"Gospel:" *Word For/Word;*

"Space Cadet 1," "Waking from the American Dream," "Mindfulness over Matters:" *North Dakota Quarterly;*

"Space Shot," "American Raspberry," and "Bubble Bath:" *BlazeVox;*

"Destination, Mindfulness:" *Sein und Werden;*

"Observatories:" *The Nonconformist Magazine.*

Troposphere

If we don't screw up the game of being human, it could last for a long time;
compared to other species, we're still early in our career.

—BILL MCKIBBEN

[F]rom the deepest agonies of the spirit.

—NORTHROP FRYE

[H]umans are precisely animals who become committed to their fictions,
adhering to them scrupulously.

—SLAVOJ ZIZEK

Launch Pad

The astronaut blue-prints from page centers,
crafting outer-space between book covers,
breaking a sound barrier into imaginative thought.
Releasing the Ark animals and flora from a pen,
the zookeeper orbits around first and last lines.

Heavenly bodies beam, extending an inch
at a time to tweak noses . . . and faces light up.
Aeronautic poets and rhyme-scheming engineers
know that the universe novel plots with humans
at blast off for the great unknown: $ABAB=MC2$.

Stuck in a zeitgeist, star-crossed readers hover
over black holes: Wheels spinning in mud.
A "slow down for children" sign flags racers.
The driver must exit from the vehicle to experience.

From the galactic margins, alien scratches re-mind
so that a new planet surprises the granted and yawn
with other places for feet and for thought.
Even in a Goldie Lock Zone the orbit stretches
at metaphor until a lie smacks Homo sapiens faces.

The thrust wakes up the fellow traveler to hope.

Space Cadet 1

Almost no matter at all   that visitors locate

                    the space station

in rural communities.   Where else?

Pumping a mountain   hollow   into a full tank,

            elbow room   into a gallon jug,

            safe distancing
                            during pandemics
into a rump gas aerosol can,

the independent isolationist   works in treetops   alone

where city entrepreneurs (millions) know
                            that money couldn't be made.

To tune in streaming through an empty field   or meadow,

a vehicle must zone out

                    while moseying all about a free way.

Zip

Sideshow and tailor mirrors
measure out joy and honesty
for the gift business in the energy field.
Hurt turns from silver, glass,
and focus enough to drive craft
into the open where the dynamo
charges the hair on a peach.

Terror backs off for another day.

Electric with cure for the masses,
two eyes light up and cheeks
press against temples: Hope may hop.

If only the honored receiver
read, reflected, and dwelt among threads,
the fitted trend-setter would see also
into vex and cave without wrinkle
how the pleats complete what seems
with a smile for a moment or a year.

A Western Bedtime Story

The space cowboy,
born all elbows with bowed legs,
straddled and jabbed upon Lacuna,
the loyal host (or parasite).
Home in the universe,
where for the galactic-buster
hoots and spurs chased thinking
with a rocket ship and a 10-gallon hat,
local planetary populations
made for a silky way.

One day, passing west through
Aporia on Main Street,
at high noon, Earth confronted,
surrounded with extinction threats
("reach for the sky partner?"),
and the conscious birth effect,
Narcissus, drew on empty holsters
and saddlebags.

Retreating from pie in the sky
to a dirty watering hole,
the yippee-ki-yay rustler sidled up
to bicycles and renewable energy
to drink someday at the bar
Clear Days Ahead.

Beyond the Spin

On the ball, the earth steward
knowing a trick never glimpses
down under foot at the luckiest
bobble in a Goldie Locks Zone.

All around the landscape tears up.
Babies bawl at the excitement.
Miners cough up coal.
Malls maul through meadows
and through mountains.
Even shorelines lose out to tsunamis.

Any confetti accumulates in waste
that poisons the atmosphere
where tomorrow-springs spring.

From the start the sun and moon
hypnotized with curiosity
where frontal lobes
stare out through socket caves.

The blue jewel that would arrest
noses for ecology and community
drained in value on the back walls
in cranium closets for neighborhoods
praying to the little dipper for a visit.

Technicians may align to melt nations
into a planet, but Stonehenge grew
into stone walls and border guards,
and the Zodiac patched an eye
with a telescope, Arrr.

Enjoy the Ride

Space travel substitutes for resentment,
regret, or anxiety about tomorrow.
Sign language, shaking a leg,
or running a shopping marathon
moves over the Earthy terrain.

The hair on a peach standing still at a bus stop
should blow back as the universe expands:
72 kilometers per second per megaparsec
—roughly 3.3 million light years.

That second hand sweeping across
a face on a wrist or on a bell tower
slaps at a moment but misses.
No flies on time but hundreds busy on the dead.

The yawn between New York and LAX
falls to sleep beneath a peopled jet-lag liner,
Oh Sippy rivers swallowing cities and towns.

The air filter with a memory minutia net
only catches onto the wails from sapiens
trying to occupy two places at once—LOL.

In the o-zone capsule cockpit smart folk relax;
thumb twiddling and cobwebs-dress-up-time
disguise so that genitalia don't disturb
with an alarm hell for the delusional.

Cricket or Cockroach Futures

On the spaceship Earth
that may lack ability
while twirling, whirling,
and hurling with a universe
(making an acrobat envious),
the astronaut learns to craft
place on the planet.
Ego and empire elbow
into tomorrow upon landfill
cradling so many creature
and human remains
that toxic lenses invite
extinction for all.
The magnetic moon
may pull at lids to blink,
but in dreams too a nightmare
in broad daylight threatens
with a brush at noses and lungs.
A monotonous mourning dove
replaces with warning
any lark or starling:
Weave latitude and longitude,
assemble berth and zone,
shape volume and venue.
No life pounces upon peace.

Night Reading

On some level, I think of the space on the page as a stage with characters
moving across.

—SUSAN HOWE

The crickets on the stage
                                        bask in evening attention
as eyes   slalom   through   silence
around   characters   and props
to denouement down at the bottom.

An emotion   heaved under
                        a meadow in an ongoing
performance to create
                                        a slippery slope for a reader
who listens for synapses and pulse.

Nestled asleep in the nervous system
                        and wow,   now on the brow
an alphabet disorder rankles
        and disturbs for the playmates.

From a first act   to catharsis
every weed whacker wishes
                                to survive the purge to inhabit
experience once . . . and again.

Adjustment in the universe,

                       where stars call out to one another
and   white fear   threatens to engulf,
sends out commas for recitation: ",,"

Imperial Crib Sheets to Shrouds

The astronaut and cosmonaut
jotted down notes on launch pads:
to dos, "b sharp," "3-2-1,"
"tomatoes," thank yous.
Throughout history, take offs
and landings happen on the fly,
Pun Fun Get Along Team.

I eye sir salutes to unity between
two empires though me and we lie;
Here come the rice and self-deception.
Both pupils planned to cheat
with orders from above
not to consider turning a cheek.

Locked innocent in battle royal
and doomed to one time capsule,
each meme sent in a saboteur stand-in
to avoid entering first beneath
the cornerstone (for easy access
to intergalactic aliens):
Dogged efforts monkeys make.

Backseat Drivers

Formal curiosity dresses in a lab coat
and either hovers over tables in goggles

or gathers in the sky through a tube
and sonar, each with augmented senses:

Findings = Top hat / tails + ceremony.

Bottom-feeding curiosity disinfects
to remove dollar signs from hands
and then gets to work on jerry-rigging
controlled disclosures to lack sacks:

Bottom-lines = Marketing champagne
(Envy donning empathy + wallet).

Need-drills organize in the streets
from toe tips to frowns to crowns

while jingles dangle dreams
at every turn: Each straight-away
and admen fashion echo chambers
on shoulders and yodel into the abysses.

Bubbles froth over a test tube;
asteroids rain into the atmosphere;
sea levels spume through cities.
Scientists sit in the backseat
on the way to town.

Sound Byte Sheet Music

Papering over contradictions,
gaps, and untruths, the bureaucrat
and business leader on ladders

with bucket, brush, and roll
align and smooth out air pockets.

The prison wall lyric loops
back to the first note on the sheet.
The inmate who at first hummed
now vomits from vertigo.

In the yard at center court
lifers living the pattern tap out
the black market for relief
from the dribbling to a basket.

The floral rhythm arrangement stinks:
Work, sleep, work, sleep - meals acciaccatura.

Across the bars the guards strum
with tin cups while sick bay frets would
trip up prisoners from other nations.
Few flourishes within the G-Clef riff
where melody tank treads roll and crash.

Scored without grace, without release,
the commuter recites with each foot planted
to and from, to and from in a chorus line.

Homo Sapiens Protocol

The psyche surgeon hunts
for emotional short-comings
and ignorance hidden
behind feigned confidence.

But first, wearing a headlamp,
the miner, armed with rolled sleeves
and a sharp brass instrument,
peels away colonies, impresses,
and biases: The parasites
that drain time and energy.

Reaching beyond immediate
pleasure principals, cornets
announce when from humiliation,
shame, and terror primal desire crowns
a second birth, a be-knighted royalty.

The womb wound inflicts to prod practice,
the praxis package that never ends.

A high chair from which to direct,
act, and edit waits
for the over-compensation master
to arrive from the audience
to surprise a species worthy.

Repeat Offenders

In the mimesis swamp,
where humans spin wheels to nowhere,
reptilian echoes haunt:
The frogs don't reel in
the flies fast enough;
eels nibble at tails
and chills wiggle up spines.

Impersonators, mentors, and models
hang around on rotting logs,
over ledges, from dead limbs.

From boredom and anxiety bubbles
fear and desire motivate
into the kingdom for hell raisers.

Miasma, the host, comes and goes
lavishing in vomiting and vertigo.
One whiff and an unicyclist
pedals to compete in the stagnant pool,
Parasite Paradiso.

A tour de France, and Indy 500
crowd in elbow to elbow, nose to nose
until tricks become cheetahs
and the unspoken rim shots backfire.
The eventual sweat tires,
bogs down the field, a tribute to Earth.

Alien Evolution

Jousting against the indifferent Goldie Luck Zone
and the local environmental cough and sneeze,
the space suit withstands for another dawn.

Breast plate, gauntlet, and air mail isolate
and brace for seeing planet Earth from inside a fishbowl.

When clubs went wild and the cheating rampaged,
senses knee-jerked at blunt imprecision
and a call went out for spades, for sharper tools.

Faking decorum until not quite making decorum
ruled for armor holding guts and bones
from death and brought to Renaissance
the light bulb, x-ray, and satellite.

The necktie, polished shoes, and skin cream
find within a peculiar posture for resistance.

Freckle, follicle and pore ally with a vertebrae legion
to back up the frontal cortex facing a sun.
The campaign weathers again and again.

Gospel

The thin-skinned evolved monkey
defines where Sirius sniffs
the dog-eared chew-toy stuck in an o-zone.
Stereo speakers repulse
should blunt instruments blow back hair.
A wrinkled forehead torches eyes
that saw no evil in a match up.

Early during the nerve-ending exposure
when calluses harnessed desire
for everything outside personal human flesh,
bulldozers and steamrollers ruled:
Peace on Earth as in the heavens.

Now, the lusty victim in a tux
on a special occasion balances
for mother and snow-capped mountains:
The giant slalom with two poles.

Late again to understand
how pulsating radio waves
and cosmic rays that crest and crash
across the universe, the ignoramus
believes in supernovas
when dark matter bloodies noses.

Neuron stars collapse into black holes
that suck at galaxy nipples on the Milky Way,
cosmic light deluges with remnant
radiation any banana lover in a tin can
romancing adventure as though
Orion tracked tender-footed lexicon loonies.

Bomb Bay Maintenance

Scuttling all truthful lived experience
for the pilots for passengers,
the Earth steward announces:
"Coffee, tea, emergency!"
The bankers in first class
navigate toward last resorts
while the uninhabitable economy hold
braces for no impact analysis.

Though the flight crew
claims to stand in for the all species
within the pressurized atmosphere,
most creatures and flora specimens
never survived to fittest.
In the cargo bay, human waste
products heap for third-world trash pickers.

Recycling streamers dangle
from the loading door, a fuselage tail
for future archeologists perhaps
or illegal intergalactic alien interest.
Stowaway indigenous animal guts
mangle in wheel wells
and on windshields, and bone-piercings
will soon adorn for the cultured souls.

Fast asleep in the overhead bin
or under a galley cart, the emissary
in apron and janitor pose
waits for the flack from the cockpit,
the missiles from the cheap seats,
the broom that leaves a planet a dust ball.

Fever

From the time capsule in the solar system
that swallows hard in a spiraling galaxy
little relief releases against
the homo sapiens virus.
Cultures grew outside Petri dishes
and so many species then died.

For dinosaurs and wooly mammoths
a universal cure slammed as though
a meteorite struck at the biological core.
For humans, green lungs cough up
suicide clouds and carbon dioxide waits
for attention outside emergency rooms.

While remaining jungles speak
in tongues, last drops drool.
The fittest on a victory lap
blankets oceans in plastic wrap,
a lamb leg or turkey breast.
Any alien can read
into the bottle for the message.

Mindfulness over Matters

The Covid-19 year-long meditation practice
medicates for true believers
sitting cross-legged, with eyes closed,
and index fingers and thumbs forming OO.

Goodbye Xanax and Lidocaine;
See ya lata Zoloft and weed.

Eastern Public Health Activation Network
recommends to all "Keep it isolated,"
body and conversation,
catching each breath alone. Ummmmmm.

The ventilators take to the streets
to scream, disrupting the quarantine routine
and the gurneyed prostrate initiative.

Having and putting down roots
in a friend forest along a consciousness
stream, from temple to temple
a sacred tele-screen flows: Pay no mind.

Should gurus chant up a vaccine
and permit talk therapy,
neighbors could travel to the far
corners in yards to Namaste and perhaps touch.

Block Parties

The bored checker board league
ticks off empty boxes each evening
when the black mark swishes overhead.
The day and date numb with numbers only.
Every wrapped gift surprises with nothing.

A checkered past stretches for great story telling
that the Everyday Convention players
never experience, can never utter about youth.
Cobwebs blurred when history
shouted out, "opportunity."

Both opponents and spectators too put to sleep
kinging coronations and checkmate threats:
A pawn inflates; a checker piece jumped.
From paper register to pixel ding
dopamine and adrenalin seeped out
into dreams and then into the galaxy.
Square sheep leap into the round meadow: zzz.

Without an energy source for a task, goal,
and purpose sublime moments and mystery
fall from refrigerator magnets
or tear from pushpin cork for posting.

Sitting at the timetable in the morning,
the map maker plots and logs for an agenda
or the game beneath sun and moon distracts
with a knight, the useful idiot.

Footpath to Identity

The love/hate relationship
with the stumbling block
trips up consciousness
every time almost.

But when the nose meets the earth
again, a particular ownership
satisfies from head to toe
among wild flowers.
A birthmark or dimple
may delight also.

And as the cosmic dancer waltzes
above and over the baited trap,
an ID badge, undisturbed,
insists with a mirror:

A sack lacking organs and bones
floats beyond silver linings,
a hot air baboon balloon.

Blue ribbons and trophies scoff.

The starting gate and headstone
and character along the way
stamp while the weather
wearer topples and skips.

Ever Glade Beat

Extracting a foot with boot
from the opinion mire tires.
No small feat . . . ..
while a simple song puts out
a million eyes with the right hook.

Truth swallows hard
but belches bubbles to the surface
to compete with lily pad lyrics.

The short-cut to wasted time
always accompanies with strings.
Marionettes tangle in unison,
hoarse at the chorus.
Finger poppers gurgle
as violence holds a note, fortissimo.
Privileged parties again look
for something more.

Depriving a reading lamp
to the imagination,
the ditty arranger grinds
to churn common ground
into a bog for ignorance.

Every prospective poet
applies to engineering school,
but after humming the bars
an escape plot emerges.

Relief

So I mean 1/3 of the food in the world is wasted but it's not profitable for
capitalism to try to sell them that food and it's not profitable to give it to them
so they won't do it.

—PETER PHILLIPS

Stockpiled unseen in shanty towns
and under mud huts,
the surplus people starve to death.
Spoon-fed by news media
to prevent privileged noses
from rubbing against nauseating images,
children aged 30, 40, 50 pretend
to not know except for lifestyle relief.

Distributing food destined for rot costs
too much for the Davos braggarts
looking for champagne splash with stolen
money that now garners other interest.

The human stash lies about
should trenches need filling
or to absorb anger from anyone
with energy enough.

Still Life: Last Exit

In chains in a trunk, the human sunk
into an unidentifiable grave.
To separate the value from the body,
banks sent in mercenaries
to mine for shadows.

A future archeologist shade
(by another "brand new" name)
may spoon out evidence
for the last three-dimensional bi-ped in earth.

In a fine fix and without breathing holes,
Houdini squirms until the worms come.
The dark dollar bills escort equals
for the echoing flesh and blood.

Without room for evolution to advance
in personal thriving spaces
celebrity assets and debt papers over
peopled culture in the halls for quiet fame.

States Department

Each day the Secretary for the Interior
registers and reports on vertical
and horizontal pressures
that threaten imagination,
free thought and speech.

(The job description comes
with security clearances
and guaranties to not be billed
for rights to a weekend constitution also.)

The shorelines, mountains, and prairies
within flesh muscle toward bone
at the sky falling and at the all-day
squeeze sites,
where envisioning
mashes against atmospheric power.

Leveraging eye candy, ear worms,
and police pistols,
the Czar from the Exterior-in-All-Matters
pries and prods to entomb dreams,
analysis, and actions.

Into depression and early death
neighborhoods on shoulders crush,
abandoning encrypted memoranda,
crumpled in memorial.

Celebrity Dream

Chasing an audience down the street,
the artist only catches up with breath,
and only when in the dust and stops running.

Alone at home, Michelangelo wrestles
with paintbrushes on a canvas
to bring to life a cultural headlock escape

while potential gallery-goers
tied to bridges by bungee cords jump
or lose consciousness on game screens,
anything but think about becoming.

The few meditators searching
for focal points stumble upon
or with antennae up on the pilgrimage
locate for an overwhelming moment.

In a studio from stone, the body builder
colors with a whole human
to fill one flesh form. . . first.

At some marker on the road to the cemetery
a backbone with eyes and a mind for growing
takes on a personal must or a child continues on.

Intersecting Logos

After fishermen mend frayed lines,
the firefighters arrive to hold
onto the network for new narrative
where passions blaze on all sides
and the fish-story-whale
leaps from the flames.

Upon the catch and then trawl haul,
meshed ropes stretch,
and some snap, as the newsworthy
headlines and tale weigh to settle
the score: crescendo . . . boom loom!

First-responder biceps and fingers
clench and lock
around circumference grips (10 to 10).

The novel age-turner ensnared
in woven hemp memory saves
for a culture future epoch truths.
The tonnage sacrifice squirming
composes to build community as runoff
facts drain from gossip heave and lattice.

Poetic Cycle

Populations looked up in the sky.
With loco motives that only spring
within heroes. . . A jet, a rocket:

Meteorite Man slammed into Earth,
blacking out the sun with dust.

Under the cloud that leaders bring
everything started to die,
so pop-eyed Know Ha, the sailor,
rounded up the surviving
fauna and flora while crafting
a space station telescope.

Quarter Master Fungshuai
orders for fresh breaths,
organizes for growing seasons.

The furniture mover rumbles
beneath feet.

Frustrated nose-ends may never meet,
never lurch beyond debate.

The great outdoors may temper,
becoming again a warning, a threat.

Room for view points
should blossom wild and awful.

When the horizons collapse
around an eye and flesh,
the metaphor beauty pageant
walks along a catwalk
while the audience consensus
chooses for the runway take off.

The Human Refreshment

After the gawking and eye-rubbing
a culture discovers through lab coats,
periodic table, and Petri dishes.
Once upon a gawk and eye-rubbing
tribes assumed through vestments, tapers, wafers.

The prop designers answer to scientists now,
where the scapegoat, guinea pig,
and two from every species
that have not yet gone extinct
travel around a sun:

Passengers and crew squeal
in an orbiting atmospheric cage.

The replaced priest and minister
plead and pray for followers
to use imaginations to form
neighborhoods, churches, congregation.
The declining stages creak and wobble
under the weigh by present tenses
and the new masks and theme music.

Victimhood adds to the pigeon
a mouse in a maze

until squinting brings onto lids
knuckle massages, re-viewing,
and the always inadequate fix.

Stratosphere

To have a conscience means to know that one is observed from a deep off-center position and pervaded by it.

—PETER SLOTERDIJK

Under Lucky Stars

Freedom dispenses from a prescribed eye-dropper.
Belonging comes in over-the-counter nose spray,
Guantanamo Bay. Aah.
The American clutches myth between the eyes
while dashing among pharmacies.

Under U. S. government surveillance,
manufacturers crank out dabs and doses
to refresh illusion on the streets
and in homes, even late at night.

Non-consumers with issues
must cough up a tissue fee,
the squeeze to catch a sneeze and wheeze.

The CCTV camera, smartphone GPS,
credit card purchase digital records
nick at close shave stories
almost causing bleeding.

The complaint that an alien moved in next door
went nowhere, as illegal as the lifestyle proved.

The application form incriminated in detail
the job candidate with potential crime to come.

At the penitentiary where debt enslaves
to guarantee labor, when salary stops
and bills pile, lifeless bodies go up in smoke.

Pirating Populations

Not a victimless crime,
privacy threatens with a thought
neighbors may not possess,
a new business model,
or an authentic way to become.
Not in sync with the city
and unwelcomed, the mind miner
sweats against the foisted title self-exile.

All memory jogging or kinking lob
perception exposes to the sensors
for inspection, or rescue squads
arrive on both eye beams
with ice picks and hallucinogens.

Pinned back for life sciences,
the frog teaches to the political elite
and the local police too: The heart pops out,
and the nerve tissues thrive enmeshed.
How reptilian legs slip through speed traps!

Every brain lines up a guinea pig
for the Internet-for-All-Things & Associates,
or a fugitive on the lam holes up, a scapegoat.

Waking from the American Dream

Mene mene tekel upharsin

—DAN. 5:25

Palm-faced until the excuse runs
as though sand through fingers,
and self-absorption, a zombie,
wanders against the traffic
on the need expressway
where shabby crowds, ransacked
and looted, pretend success.

On green patches not yet privatized
families prop up the economy
with tent poles.

With a tickle here and a tickle there
reptilian brains march on stiff legs
toward craving, want, and greed.
Even the hedge fund giant
drools over the next new prospect.

When mimetic desire lifts a feather,
only a second nature well-trained
in determined conscience
enters the streets with stubborn placards.

Three hundred years of science crowds out
the independence that declares self-blame.

Ringtone Tune

At home in the phone,
where the dear and the emoji
interplay, a renter puts up feet
on an image processor
and lets down hair
for a corporate owner
and stockholder friends.

The personal mirrors two-ways;
the private pirated for fortunes.
Hard at work to obtain
a sanity pause,
elfie selfies coughs up
the monthly statement fee.

The coltan sapiens
rises in the morning
beside mattress and pillow
in cramped quarters.
The workday among keys
and apps soon amputates
from the waist down: waste.

Any eccentric gene,
all experiential twists,
every snowflake claim,
peels off, flesh, from the carrot.
No need for a shtick or stick.

Fee, Fi, Fo, Fum a giant
in a cloud grinds at bones
to bake and break bread.

Every Thing, a Nail

The imprisoned zookeepers gatekeep:
Dogs, chickens, geraniums - specie survivors.
Linear cranium mining helped
to craft the bars, the boxes,
the projection onto fauna, flora, terrain
whether static, dynamic, weather.

The global imagination deforestation project
grunted out manmade deserts
(roots and all) to build mansions
for the self-selected few.
Had the weed-pullers squeezed among
the trees to sandwich
more generous offerings to the earth,
Earth might would have been.

However, shouldacoulda chugged into the past.

Along the xylophone cage,
inmates with tin cups bang and clang
for loose change or for the next meal.
Within every home (or worse, tent),
each hostage and jailbird lifer
smiles when an emoji plants.

B Sharp, Fortissimo

A pre-tongue lashes at the nimble-footed
blank page (look look) until a membership
harbors an interest in a local memory bank.

A rue revolutionary, the poem by and for
overthrows T to constitute parties to form
a whole where a hole represented: Hip hip . . .
"One if by land; two if by sea."

The mime at the keyboard bangs out
the melody for one solo audience, perhaps two.

Violins gather about "A;"
a bird feathers in the alphabet.
Abutting anxiety between flowers,
with buzz beeing props up worlds.

Coke, the Real Thing

From sugar high to sugar high,
the money interests rely on
the democratic state to motivate
even the poets and philosophers.
The powdered donuts and chocolate
bars feed a carrot promise
for a horse giddy up.

The laborer and bureaucrat whinny
while keeping score on television
and at the polls, no matter who wins.
Rhymers know to put feet between lines
on Sundays between two and four only.
The ponderer never wants to escape
the grotto found in party politics.

A Yankee walks down any street
in the world, a global glob
in exceptional latex leggings,
a reminder to the domestic workers
that liberty need not flee a pursuer:
"High everyone."

The corn-starched mustache and
slave mentality, armed (out-performed
by shoes that stamp equal signs
with every step toward tyranny) weighs
to impress along the gone American way.

The Foot Instinct

The poet knew by rote
that Styx and the stone
would stain and absorb a life,
crisp naming and the blotter.

After the recital, Homers wrote
with gravity and only now
return to the lung.

How many rock climbers
clambered before to create the reflex?

The difference blathered and spilled
onto pages that needed tension
more than attention from others.

Since paper caught a breeze
where pixels come and go,
tongues wag to the fore.

Until the truth thief piles up
all the lies for children to see
and honesty adhesive holds
enough for humans
pores sweat in metaphor.

Toast

No joke, the philosophy egg center,
with all the physics and hardened logic
cradling, cracks and breaks into the world
with cheap cheer or sets on the table:
hard boiled, soft boiled, sunny side over.

The rotting need for decision
ticks away at the good but not the evil
that sizzles bacon on a griddle.

For brains that eat the bodies beneath
the picket fence and rose garden camouflage
along the infamous bread crumb trail:
The cosmic eye and jaundiced brow marry.

Children cluck at stoics throwing
chicken feed around or the backyard
grows more and more quiet, yoked
to fat privilege enjoying another parenthood.

In galactic Chaos, where justice jostles only,
little falls to beggars from clutches with arms
unwilling to grasp responsibility
by the customized handle.

The 21st Century Limited

A blunt instrument with multiple registers
and intricate detailed noting possibility,
the conscience whistle quits before a tweet
when corruption lip-services the public:
20-years in solitary for one blow;
stars show up everywhere for the community.

A canary dead in a nation.
A gas-lighted mob chugs along the ideology track
(without klaxon peal, without bell), a diesel engine
mowing down any body not onboard:
Edward Snowden, Chelsea Manning, Julian Assange.
The constitutional flute player chased after breath
when the air sucked from spacesuit and helmet.
Thanks to the oblivious supporting cast,
blind to the violence that ignor-ance wreaks.

Olive Branch Bunch

While religions and peoples compete
with guns, missiles, and resentment, vultures circle.
The heart-sleeved throbs for a world without cultures.

The fist without knuckles knocks at the door
to the amygdalae or at least beats
upon the frontal lobe shelter.

The cooperation conglomerate shares in dreams.
A hope diamond twinkles among inner-spaces.

A table for enemies to talk around
brooms animosity from the room:
and the meek call due the big stone owed.

Seeking shoe plumbers, empathy pumpers
peace-sign using a pen and two separated fingers
(index and middle).

The deed done names with chest bumps.

Momentum Memento

On holidays the train wreck
sits around the table: The engine, smoking
or steaming (or both) with embarrassment
over the embankment;
off the rails, zigzagged cars
with windows staring at the sky;
the beads in the compartments lie rattled,
dazed and moaning, unconscious, or worse.

Though the kitchen delights with roasts
and with herbs added to the gravy and greens,
though the relatives arrive on time
and chitchat when the host exhausts,
though the place setting imperatives impress
and champagne bubbles for all
(without the accordion music),

the first responders wail
until all the gurneys are loaded
and the emergency vehicles have arrived
at the hospital emergency rooms.
Only at that moment does the next generation
begin to race against time and space on Earth
with greater ferocity than any role models.

Requiem Retro

The long-playing record,
(keeping score, logging trivia)
fiddling with a lifetime on edge,
tucks into shelving, and after
a short while, forgotten.

Grooves, some scratched and rutted,
needled into self-consciousness
and sometimes compassion,
pique into momentary satisfaction.

The music in repeated experience
climaxes for the musician and listener.

Round and round the Earth goes
for speakers and ears, harmonizing
in soon old-fashioned species.

Without winner and only losers,
the treadmill breaks into a run,
hi-fi into high five without reason.

Memory founders under brain dust
throughout the living room
where now accords to wall shadows.

Gullible Travesty

Ulterior motives catch on an upper lip,
snaring naivety and the long-delayed startle,
or lodge in the gullet complicating escape,
a fool mounted on a wall in a den
or tossed to sure scavengers.

The hook casts into an ear, music,
dropping into cavities a long G note,
but the bait never splashes into the belly
even when the dancer dangles, pirouettes.

The networker and fly-by-night domino
soloist lines up possible winning futures,
a default mechanism at work stands,
while charging the expense to others
without concern for datelines, fall-guys all.

A manipulated slacker slug, three days old,
appears in the newspaper under pinched noses
that witness ta-dum-da-dum-dum-dum.

The Resound Landlord

What it claims as its own is the depth of a person's inner life. . . .

—GEORG WILHELM FRIEDRICH HEGEL

Claiming ownership over inner-life also,
music notes to confront and measure
living room and then moves
to collect rent among bodies.

At the automotive garage where
functional architecture reflects
the boot camp reflex training

the penny pinching boarder performs
for the short-term reason and no rhyme,
surfaces serving habit until into a cemetery.

Encountered by only roar and silence,
the tenant assumes that veneer mechanics
fill interiors with blessing and bliss.

Should ears whorl into blossom
before lungs sag into snore,
mood moves in waving a deed,
and feet turn into metaphors.

Violins drag about affect furnishings:
a brass section pointing out,
a ribcage atmosphere embracing birds,
the heart beat and flutter, 4 by 4.

Flight AAA 2020

[I]f you do that you then have to forfeit the fraudulent myth of the sovereign
Alpha American who can take care of himself . . . you'd have a little bit of
foam on the runway.

—DYLAN RATIGAN

Seated in economy class
on an Alpha American Airline,
the workers and unemployed brace
for impact and the buckling to come.

On the runway no foam greets,
no emergency apparatus, no ambulance
anticipates where the bodies will land.

Listening for the belly beneath the beast
to crunch, burst, and screech,
the heads between knees watch for
barf bags sliding under seats in front
while overhead bins thunder.

On the observation deck
in the air traffic control tower
the social engineers nod off in time
to deny knowledge, to claim
ignorance, to cry "collateral damage."

Trapped in a country skidding
into wreckage, individuals,
who manifested destinies into nightmare,
react to cabin pressures and jet fuel,
and to bounding scapegoat baggage,
—the almighty dollar axed
from budgets decades ago.

The Buried Alive

In the retirement community
newly minted poets and painters
claw at grave walls dug decades ago
for corporations, practices, and firms
that relieved adolescent anxiety.
The largest rocks in the solar system
pile onto shoulders rounded
by gravity and years and years
within empty evenings.

Atlas with a tissue dabs at brows
in pity even though eyes sheltered
against Sisyphean purpose punishment.
The child who opens to the vast
terrorizing muse becomes to brace
for a vulture dining on a liver.

Eighteen manicured front lawns
for pretending that a ball in a hole
could plug the universe;
the wrinkles in the thinking
expose at the last ditch.
Perhaps penning symbols
for grandchildren obfuscates
enough to teach lay from lie
in cities and suburbs owned
by the walking dead.

Show Trial

When reputation tanks due
to a breakdown in systemic
propagation or cover,

money launders with PR lawyers
jiujitsuing for the defense
in the public square.

Scrubbed in victimhood,
the violence enacted by a thug
hangs out back, ghosts
wearing clothespins on noses.

Angels who suffered since
childhood, mothered by violins,
display on screens and in ears
up and down the streets

until tears flow in an operetta
for the brute and the injured
casts in a nameless low-life role.

Shipbuilding on the High Seas

While waves lift and drop design features,
ship resources remain with hands at hand.
On a deck that gouges at water
day and night the stars wait
for winks while eyes act as suns.
Philosopher charms, Sloterdijk and Zizek,
tattooed onto forearms, warm with hope.
In the streets tomorrow crews endure
while learning ongoing shipbuilder trades
where yesterday police
spy, mace, beat, and shoot.
Carried away with the wind gusts,
the to-do list lists and reinvents
with every current event and upheaval.
From side to side quarters
for a captain shifts for one long stand up,
jostling jolting jokes all about a helm.
With the future in mind and a sextant
in a death grip the wrights wield and weld,
plug and pipe, chalk and calk
until bulge and rudder calm sea legs
that lug and tug toward a more perfect union.

All Systems Go on the Potter Wheel

The astronauts   on the Third Stone   space craft
reach out to one another   and barely touch.
With gratitude the evolved monkeys sigh
at any connection at fingertips.

Harmonizing behavior codes   in room enough,
sol stewards watch for pitch,   listen for bounce,
assisting fellow choir members   who swing and twirl.

Interior states and organ representatives report
on mind and body functions: All A OK.
Roger everywhere,   from toes to nose.

Oceans wave,   sending friendly tidings
from frozen poles,   from re-assured shores.
Mice and manes and fins feather in instinct.
Exhausted dinosaur ghosts   that once roared by
from tailpipes rest in peace . . .   again
finally with rust heaps in junkyards.

Having survived the planet pruning,
rocket scientists debated   and won
against CEOs   so space cadets could climb
into the nose cone cockpit
        to smooth out the spin   and travel
into the unknown   gaps   among stars.

Mesosphere

The images that our deep observer sends us speak a clear language.
They speak to our conscience regarding Earth.

—PETER SLOTERDIJK

Current Event

Circling the drain
just outside universities,
brains whir and gush
to distant lands where
surroundings respect
the arts and sciences
and arts and sciences
respect surroundings.
No stopping with cork,
police state, or seduction.

Patching pants and work week,
the exhausted main street
hustler wallows in shadows
for hedge fund and corporate
managers in pressed shirts.

                  The vortex takes
with future generators
                                 the clocks and health:
              Baby and bath water.
Trumped and twisted
                        one last twirl to stagnate
            atmosphere, corruption
buys up the busy bodies
                     running among multiple
          low-wage, part-time jobs.

The deliberate hands
paddle toward tomorrow,
the flushed faces learning
new languages smile.

A School

At the us Navel Academy,
everybody studies to become
a commander from berth to front door
in the overnight shipping order dept..

A gaze haze camouflages
so that animals appear gullible
to pet or erase, and flora charms
all homing desires for knots around.

Twisting the high seas to reflect
a child screaming in excitement
and replace any moment for inner states,
tenor trauma entreats for the space cadet.

Once rock replaced a man on a lawn
outside a library and warmed
spinal column cockles in any foyer,
entering into life support proved useless.

Practice Makes

Hard-landing on the American continent,
the space craft from the Enlightenment
cracks along the United States.
A dreamed more perfect union,
glued together by ideals squirted out
from a Constitution tube and dried
between institutions, exhausted
within day-to-day struggles by 1970.

Fifty small nations surfaced
from sea to shining sea.
Topographers outlined in bold ink
and pixels for tourists, vagabonds, refugees.

When from the blue the sun enshrines
for each homo sapiens potential, natures
may not run for life against a barbarian.
In the nose cone atop such a paradigm ship
the praxis human learns to fail better
as a steward loving the arts among stars.

Rounding Up Democracy

Captured by impersonators,
the muzzled office holders
put on a good show for each other
in the jailhouse, surely some song and dance.

Ventriloquists and puppet masters
look for work elsewhere.

Look-alike actors listen to Main Street,
then put in orders for ball and chain companies
while calling soldiers "The Police."

At the voter Live Meat and Great Grate,
the imposters serve thick bologna sandwiches
and cheese whiz smiles all around.

Pleased with the straw poll
and the take-home pay left after extraction,
the straw man wins a pole for a spine
alone in a field with blackbirds.

The contorted wealthy stakeholder faces
own own, while the governed audience
groans and moans searching
for empty refrigerator boxes.

Rocky, the Moved

From Cyclopic peaks,
granite navigates straight down
into fear and desire without drowning
where over centuries tidings
wash away mountain feet.
Mica-might erodes into grotto grit
or hollow hello hell. However,
stone may learn to swim in emotions.

When the day comes that the shale shell
plops into anxiety, and affect wakes
and sprouts from shoulders and hips,
limbs flail not to fail: Head above no reflex.

Breathe, while the dog paddle struggles
through panic, but the panting
begs for more than hounding horizons.

Eventually, the slapped together splash-work,
relaxes into surgical strokes for kicks
and moods swell into buoyancy.

The sink or grin lesson ends
with discovering the flotation flesh
huffed and puffed with passion and sense,
a monument to movement.

Knowledge to Bear

Reflexes tent for decades in a library
reference room to prepare for the bias test.
Even then nerve-ending bundles escape
from exercise routines daily:
Top shelf calisthenics, how-to passages,
and theme spirits miss out on a nose
and heart sleeping in for look-alikes.
Midnight oil fury fails to keep up
the worst students who, exhausted, fall
behind Oxford English Dictionaries
but arrive with fresh daisies to the church
fair for cheeky preemptive strikes.
Prejudice, racism, xenophobia, sexism,
the vents for status slippage and shame
howl with violence all around the scapegoat
who brings peace and a justice finally.
At an altercation altar mobs, who dignify
the homo sapiens, beg for the CRSPR,
and ignorant scientists listen and map:
If it can be done, it must be done.

Mooning at the Glitter

The poet rattles at cell doors,
sucks on a binky, and cries
when nursery rhymes end.
The Bastille cellar brat
prays for each foot
to twinkle in the night sky
when the menu offers
only dirt for every meal.

From motherhood get-go
mutation limitation eats
at future balladeering flesh.
Each song leads to a gong,
and the reader still in
merely a little older skin.
Desire for development
invents until a denial basket
floats down the Nile
or brainwashes upon
the Mississippi banks.

With fingers plugging at
the keys in seeming Everland
the hermitage construction
built from spores and bacteria
grows up a cellular type A-Z
personality that punctuates
an organism wishing
on the spaces between the stars.

Performance Memorial Services

When sitting in the director chair,
the past exposes to the actor
what wasn't known at the time
along with selective segments
from what was understood.

Memory wakes up the movie star
playing a role in a burlesque show
with understudies nowhere in the wings.

When the victim/bruiser monster
appears, the creature who never asked
to arrive or to take part, disguises,
smoothing on the Human salve,
to stop the itch and scratch.

All the while, the improv goes on,
and the Defense Surveillance
viewer hisses, sniggers, guffaws.

Disaster Master

Tragedy averted, muscles from chin
to ears stretch until teeth appear.
Catastrophe-overwhelmed,
a body slackens until rigor mortis sits in.

Oars and a dinghy choke off paradise islands
from the struggle to satisfy desire.
Any shore becomes sure.
The leash law by-product rescues
for tomorrow with a wink
and again the monotonous growl
wolfs up breathing-time for one more day.

The school for happiness strokes
to harbor all the hard labor: "Good buoy."
The fetching-after buy-products
and a paste-on smile pose
the biggest questions:
If a laughter sags in the middle,
what ointment anoints?
If the howl games the hunt,
why hound the pound?

The joy ploy toys,
while the thrive-striver survives.

Socratic Book-Keeping

Bellying up to the past,
the accounting firm Zero-Sum Game
thirsted to align preaching
with praxis for the records.

Shots from decades ago lined up
on the bar chased by a frosted mug
who exhibited for mercy upbringing,
schooling, and culture in defense.

The photos reddened all around
where cheeks, perched on stools,
exposed empathy . . . or identity.
Adult character traits, grown
from yesteryear, marveled
but didn't swoop to rescue.

Mr. Gloss glances from the mirrors
where stubble, once details shaved clean,
wattles on a now dropped jaw.

Staggered by the deep drafts
from a youth play book and spreadsheets,
the drunk at Know Thyself Lounge
and Grill braces at the doorway out
and pleads for gin, vodka, scotch.

Being Territorial Claims

The back turns away from wherever
both eyes come together.

Importance agreements zoo-in
zoom lenses and k-9s.

The perspective that gathers
behind the head calls out a name,
but focus distracts from the hailing.

Ears, nose, pores salute in one direction
while the alerts alarm from another, unnoticed.

And under the skin-lids a fear fortress
sends out search and destroy patrols
to protect the ignorant citizen.

The blind dot that captures few imaginations
marks off parameter perimeters,
a country, continent, an era with royalty
ordering and directing each actor
thought by thought and foot by foot.

Unless a surprise guest turns around fast
to crash the projection campaign party,
the peasant in a field for study
misses out knowing the ass plowing ahead.

Measure Twice, Cut Once

In the gap between
scientific curiosity and technology
deliberation blooms before
impulsive stepping or staying.
The garden for speculating outcomes;
the orchard for imagined alternatives;
and fields for open spaces exploration
and educated second guesses
grow on and on for nation states.

The damned footing "If one can,
one must" skips over thought, logic,
assessment, cracking open
skulls and spilling entrails:
A child plays with explosives.
Every species on the planet writhes
over a half understood experimental
forecast and the itch by one humanoid
for a money-making entrance.

On the innovation track,
bound for fame in finance,
the robotic impress rolls while a planet
becomes stuck in sludge.

Honesty Font

Shoulder to shoulder, neck on neck,
sculpted from salt, and fed
by wounds that only close slowly,
the tear fountain stands at a place
in time, making private public
without scapegoat ceremony.

Tourists from long practiced
cold attitudes sit around on a lip
with pennies for wishing but never
staying to learn the intricate style,
the briny taste, the same-boat behavior.

In pairs, possible parties to a mob
refuse to show up at the square
with torches, pitchforks, and rope
since admitting to participation in all.

Even in daylight and under brave
evening lamps the interstellar emptiness
fills for springs in chests and wells up
into the personal matters at hand.

Interlocking upper-limbs
on a foreign body, two cisterns
drain from eyes to share the loads
bent on memory and understanding.

Tai Chi to the Promised Land

Around the globe on a good day
rainforests and oceans inhale and exhale;
behind the pipers animals follow.
All in one breath, the lung enablers
chant and hearts beat: Organism
harmonics, organism harmonics.

Every class and species, genus and ilk
practices at aum and ah, or dies.

When cough and choking interrupt
the meditation on planetary planted plants,
oil threatens to add mammals to fossil
deposits, frogs and birds to coal veins.

The cynics at the gas pumps, competing
with developing countries melt poles
and raise all boats, forgot that leadership
in anusara brings home Namaste and Gesundheit.

Photosynthesis from the lotus pose
opens up osmosis and cherry blossoms
for walking a mile in shoes from the closet.

20/20 Vision

In the greenhouse, young corporate
candidates ripen into elite smug-ignorance
on the lobby vine and on campaign trails.
Around the bend on a hill a white house
fertilizes and waters with history books.

Americans vote for nature
but live in disinfectant bubbles.

To pick an organic tomato not under glass,
radical taste buds need to bloom.
And only extreme weather, poisoned people,
debt-enslaved unemployed graduates
possibly blossom into placard-petaled streets:

Hong Kong throng, Moscow minion movement,
an Arab spring ring with crocus for peace
jarring the DC shock and awe windshields
and the NYC and LA la-la bell jars.

Between where the wild things scar
and hegemony doesn't care,
ideas enlighten to cultivate for a garden.

Carrion Song

Citizens self-censor for CCTV
documentary series Human Life Patterns
and for GPS capture devices,
playing Fred and Ginger during commutes
while sleepwalking into despotism.

Enthralled in the opportunity to be seen
each performer without costume
or back stage or at rehearsal drones on and on
until algorithms zzzzzzzzzzzzzzzz.

The poet, whose job description states
"warn the people" writes for editors
who don't live under desks
and possible readers busy paying off debt.

Using cameras, ear-buds, and incentives
shapers nudge and mould into cemeteries
to allow the Homo Deus species births
without sapient fear, protest, or riot.

Damp from spittle the clarion call
molders and rots before eyes find
and after a genus corrupts unless
something more than alarm
invests in numbed nerve endings.

Western Hemisphere Adult Education

With an undiagnosed military industrial complex,
the useful idiot holes up in a basement bunker
eating canned psychology and a dried Eisenhower Era
beef and sipping from a shiny TINA canteen.
The expert in a dunce cap waits to wise up
while the reinforced concrete media, Ayn Rand library,
and camouflage paint the united state.

Outside, Schadenfreude dams up allies, friends,
and the relative ease that once allowed Ahab to shoot
fish in a barrel while talking block party politics.

The boomerangs pivot over shrinking oceans,
over border walls, and over defense contracts.
In a too-late dream, manufactured cows graze
and derricks drill on the passing thought
"Avenue MLK/RFK" that never moved
off the childhood drawing table.

Hate grows on family trees in the many bombed out
distant lands mined beneath homes.
Once blindfolded Boston suburbanites lined up
against plastic straws where irony may soon surprise.

Cry from a Planet

The substitute,
guffaws and giggles,
carries for a face
through main streets
and back quarters
and into bed each day.
Resting a whole head
on the philosophy
stuffed inside irony
and not on a sponge
allows for sleep without
the quaking in waking.

The loft interior
crows a skylight and beats
wringing out a pillow
each morning.
The information age police
slap on smiles for application
in household palms
and inspect for adhesive
routinely at traffic signals.
In an attitude/attribute park
amusement stands out
among clowns.

At media check points
in commercial districts
marketers frisk for frowns.
The sophist, who plans
for catastrophe comets
and planetary sun burn,
learned to toddle as a babe.

Bank Vault

Capital Darwinism lines up scavengers
on cliff ledges and in the tree tops:
Hedge fund cleanup craws
and credit card packs maul.

No experts, no witnesses surveying salary
infusions slowing to stop in debt for death.

The howl or caw welcome into the kingdom
though outsiders need not, actually.

For two-legged desire chasers,
reason, imagination, and love
may have rescued from predators.

A more universal dream could have
populated for all species
where carcasses now sprawl rotted.

No archeologist brushes
at mammoth wallet fossils.

Instead, at the mine mouth
for the human resource department
gold bricks trump into silence
as though the cockroach were all, ever.

Survivalist Retort

Business plans and public relations knuckles
shake in the faces that hold breaths
to save Earth from cultural climate crises.
The fist frisk in the threatening nature
absconds with clean air and water
and the cent at pocket bottoms.

Rattled at birth, a lone crybaby in a hospital
nursery howls at the moon.
The birth control method chops up cribs
and playpens for firewood to warm elderly
off-duty Walmart greeters.

The "damn life," survival-for-the-fittest-magnates
look to other planets, other solar systems,
and hole up in 1950s missile,
or family farm wheat, silos.
Telepathic telescopes take root in corneas
peering through The Wall Street Journal.

Waiting for the green-alien-power-plant-teams
to arrive with seeds at last to boot-up the earth,
science friction experts send out smoke signals.

Thermosphere

What the myth tells us is that the Tower of Babel is a work of human imagination, that its main elements are words, and that what will make it collapse is a confusion of tongues. . . . It never speaks unless we take the time to listen in leisure, and it speaks only in a voice too quiet for panic to hear. And then all it has to tell us, when we look over the edge of our leaning tower, is that we are not getting any nearer heaven, and that it is time to return to the earth.

—NORTHROP FRYE

Poetry is the original letting-dwell.

—MARTIN HEIDEGGER

Climate Climax

For a human being,
SUCK for venom and spit
to take the sting from a bee.
Introduce with all CAPS
but plan for anticlimax.
An S with fangs snakes
around town to deflate the alarm.
The ladder, engine and rescue squad
swarm about a cat in a tree.
"The situation could have been worse:"
An old sweet song
written by a philosopher.

However, should the sun
beat up skyscrappers
and gridded street fighters
or sea water top off already
stilted houses with people inside,
scientists jump up and down
on granted funds: no fun.
Money makers roll eyeballs
and jingle small change.
Solar System Pequod
doesn't turn on a dime
or for a silver dollar.

Destination, Mindfulness

The now horizons pinch
at the hobo shivering under
the momentary extraction stars
mining resources, raw material
from a live body sitting
in an automobile in traffic.

Local histories, reflections,
and legends house redundant
in a cloud or in a tiresome
silicon memory board
while each morning blank slates
from screens and ear buds
distribute with coffee.

Tomorrow, another spotlight
arrives without an audience
and the sky fracks, guts
from head to toe—ta-da.
AI with an eye just for fun
sweeps up into a dust pan
after the IT jujitsu move on beings.

With yesterday a bruising blitz
and with a to-do list streaming
through pixels the bum in park
on the freeway has never been at home.

Dwelling

The relentless brightsiders
and the drive-by hope killers
dismember eyes from thought.
Should the duo team up,
dizzy could tip over a country,
a planet with the slightest push, dominos.

A quiet, determined now
under noses walls out
silver linings and parading
balloon poppers whenever
single-minded pupils calibrate.

Once the moment startles
open the frontal lobe,
the whole cerebellum,
including the amygdala,
realizes into people, pets,
and trees until options
encompass inverted possibilities.

Maps that lead to wilderness residue
(orchards, arboretums, national forests,
the junkyards for the useless and the token)
unfurl for trailblazing away
from domination nations.
Backtracking—a joke.

The short-lived biped hack quakes, wakes,
without window dressing,
to brave lights against the black,
sky beyond a sun.

Dead Ahead: Easter Island

The flight to Easter Island from Discomfort,
a state that suffers shifting baseline syndrome,
wore out an ecosystem in order
to rest everything on cushions and pillows.

To have banked to the left or to the right
when first fleeing, would have water-logged
a whole population in drink:
Jameson, Smirnoff, Budweiser oceans.

Too late to turn back, the Western World
plows around the planet on the belly
into tomorrow, soil poisoned from yesterday:
Pesticide, herbicide for suicide.

So much for a conquering nature.

Every culture born, a sucker that fails
to meet the solar system challenge.
To knot too early the rise to cooperate
with an indifferent atmosphere
chokes off airports and birth rates.

Culture Climate Change

Dressed in camouflage and later
each evening returning to a cell,
the steward wonders among
the fauna and flowering.

Not inmate or monk,
but no narcissus anymore,
the Goldie Flock Zone
resident sweats, for now,
to balance . . . "just right."

At first, the flower child
and animus admirer
on a see-saw responded
to the surrounding
please pleas with jokes:
Who came first chicken,
egg, or farmer Jones?

Conspicuous consuming
and envy-waste warred
against the poor, blaming
starvation on hunger.
Slums choked on self-loathing.

The culture climate changed
when hopelessness challenged
windpipes and Homo sapiens
lungs could not find oxygen enough
without trees and seed couriers.

Higher Education for All

At Futile University,
students learn from experience
that the cosmos ignored
100 billion morons who came before
and will do the same to the today-stars.

No tassels and mortarboards don
regardless the Nobel and Carnegies,
but if lucky and rain washes necks,
green grass grows all around, all around.

To free desire from family and friend best wishes
and the security forces who pledge
to pursue deserters to issue whim grants,
the hassle torments with mornings, noons, nights.

Sometimes a vehicle for love pulls up
in a neighborhood to drive play at work
and a ne'er-do-well imagines fanfare
for a hero and whisks to better humanity.

After the parties drinking
the ice-cap course taken at the offering,
the climate change grilling,
the third degree slacker fatalities harness
to gurneys for an examination
by any survivors.

Wholly Cow!

Sliced from an intent wheel,
Swiss garnishes best
with lettuce and tomato.
A generous ham with a wit spread
stretches out on a seeded wheat field.

The worker hums
with a "Yum" at lunchtime.

Ignoring the holes (chance,
Luck, emergency) in the drive
to achieve the big "cheese" photo,
the curd weigher counts on thumbs up
without plum or favoritism.

But sometimes a seeming forever
rabbit burrow carries for no reason
. . . an Alice falls into an Oz.

More udder fool than den rodent,
the determined churner
often ends up delighting
over a deli delicacy

whether exposing strength,
a nutty sweet riddle alone,
or sandwiched in partnership
with China shop bulls
or fate finessers.

Welcome

With every step,
loneliness turns and tumbles
between insole and foot bottom,
a rock between a hard
place and tender flesh.
From ball to pinky,
grit to pearl, blisters churn
into boot leather.
Worn out before worn out,
Polished hide empties
to nothing and to denying
the gravity, pebbly paths
to hide against.

Shod in calluses,
a pointed isolation riles
within each community member.
Encrusted alienation
strikes out with misplaced anger
and falls in love
with innocent liars.
Only pumas stone, Earth-size
breaks down each thug.
Mis-takes try to reach
out to mis-takes;
No winners laurel
the trophy case.
Drool in nursing homes
moves up from ankles, blossoms.

Arbitration Nations

More perfect unions
among the united spaces
float in ether contingency
within heads that consider options.
Topographic puzzle pieces
or, bolder, shoulder to shoulder
attention spans pinch
for most Yea sayers
and observant comfort seekers.
A wedge issue vice seams
along with other good ideas
for states caught in the middle:
seafood miff or continental drift.
Missouri and Illinois
scream out "Mississippi."
Austria and Switzerland
laugh at little but each other.
And Tibet! Where in hell? . . . Tell.
The sandwiched meat meets
during rush hour, underground,
and between stations
in subway cars, and coagulates
to imagine salami. (Slim chance.)
Shoving off to roam,
the caper cadet scopes out rough
terrain without compass or map
to climb over backyard fences.
Arm-in-arm real estate buffoons
picket foreclosure rates.

The American Raspberry

In a field   with feet planted   in broad daylight

the organic farmer shouts out   the American gain

to eyeballs   glued to dollars.

Behind optic nerves,   a dopamine hawk tips   on a limb

          expecting movement below.

Each   seeded row   producing   for   personal   growth   a
community

rots at harvest   while debt slavery whips   through lifetimes

leaving bold thought erased,   lobes fallow,   walls   without
bookshelves.

Only fingers that skate across   the phone chirp

feel for Braille,   any sign in glass,   reflection or fish below.

Slick propaganda bytes   nibbling pupils and nimble thumbs

while sliding watches   into cemetery plots.

No loafer inhales   and on summer grass   corrugated cardboard

wakes at mowers copping   hieroglyphic green space for no one.

A garaged wheelbarrow   listens for the language discoveries.

Poetic Loupe

While history strings peril pearls
interstellar loneliness reaches out
for stone and stick
to hold dialogue with darkness
through practice and a tool.

The empathetic irony in graphite
marks upon each day until a habit,
coaxing from silence, performs physics.
Listening to night through blue sky,
speech parts from influence rain:
ears whorl into grasping fingers.

Mollusk metaphors bead into epochs,
each singing about grit and salt,
cultivating arcs, reasons that fit the fits:
Hellenic, Roma, Stratford-Upon-Avon.

The chord that threads compressed
variations on an emblem carries
to commune and feed for a shell
where poets wrestle in mud.

Only the fish-eyed jeweler
schooled in what looms and dooms
pierces with the wanting a line
that defines the planets by name.

Language Gains

You won't see something that is common to all, but . . .
a whole series of [similarities].

—LUDWIG WITTGENSTEIN

Family resemblances and expressions
fade into oblivion without rave
reviews or much criticism.
Inherited wealth, if any,
or a rocker that cradled a grand
somebody stand creaking against time.

And genes, what passed on,
(that didn't pass on with a corpse)
spring with a nose from nowhere
or a cognitive short-cut
that birth abnormal responses
from friends, strangers, and enemies.

So much for an imagination
to crowd in 110 billion, and counting,
souls orbiting (a halo?) around Earth.
Blessed sad Saturn must have been
unaware that a twin resided
in the solar system with seven
other siblings (and a bastard)
waiting for warmth from a hot mama.

Would-be astronomers and astronauts
line up to question galaxies and compare
stars for planets from afar: poets all.

Temple Logic

Under the knowledge tree
that bears atomic fruit on limbs
reaching out to progress for millennia,
monkey progeny shelter
while Bikini Isle guinea pigs pave
a way to green light mushroom clouds:
Twelve-Year Daily News—Bravo!

The scientist searches and researches
so that each Jack Horner pulls out a plum
to focus on. Next door, Dr. Jackal
presents to arsenals isotopes for dopes.

Chomping into tomorrow
with gulpible hopes, a Capitol boon
may or may not nourish much
when digesting a new, improved mush
with booming improv cemeteries.

Kneeling at the life-altering concept altar,
the alimentary canal in a birthday suit
might consider investing right, rite,
and time in Rainbow Ark fleets, calling out
to evolved ministry, choir, congregation,
"Please, please, please green peace."

Now You See . . .

The blind spot for the Enlightened rabble
erases on Earth, and indigenous people disappear.
Just below rouser status on the goader chart,
the reformers occupy and steal for "good."

The global impressed parchment topsoil
speaks to close readers, pathfinders, archeologists.

Listening with eyes and finger tips
to the hollows, valleys, and shallow graves,
imprint diviners hunt for another extinct species:
Tohono O'odham, Nicarao, Yaaku, Bikini, Assam.

Empire narcissists rub out and check off lists
for a library one hundred years later.

With telescope, microscope, pillowed chair
the crafty culture drifters and resource hoarders
cut-corners on creature comforts for the host at home.
When the engineered genes come on the scene,
the Best in the West natural parasite, look out!

Observatories

Once upon a planet only lids opened up
to search in the heavens for heaven
or a place to land a tin can.

Now so many worried eyes in the sky
size up every corner on Earth
where envy punches down at empathy.

When conscience might beat hearts,
sockets fall to reptile impulses.

The cooperation that threw a tube
carrying beings at the moon sits fated
on a launch pad, a deflated hot air balloon.

Wind blows across deserts where wildlife
preyed in lush flora and across the faces
left behind for poised, rag-tag reasons.

Too few pupils dilate from brainstem
to frontal lobe to bring honor to Homo sapiens.

Lift Off

After the rabble rumbles
and the rubble bounces on the spaceship,
space craft rules:
Sentiment sediment settles.
Waste station retro-rockets,
sanded elbows, and shoe horns
jitterbug on negotiated floors.

Where hubris bubbles up to suffice,
each face in the fishbowl magnifies
in an ozone space helmet.

Jamming musical instruments
and lemons squeeze in.

Angels gather on a pin head
for hair-splitting mathematics.

The artisan with a tape measure
and yard stick for rapping knuckles judges
to sack stuffers suffering big plans.

Honoring the room taken up by organs
in other than human organisms, a totem stands:
Lions, buffalos, and bears, oh my!
"This land is made for" them,
indigenous people, and me too.

Camouflaged rubs and brushes
and wide open places –
make way, make way starlight, star bright.

Portrait: Space Shot

... [O]uter space has allowed us to succeed in representing the external
partner of conscience.

—PETER SLOTERDIJK

Empathy on empty and conscience
addicted to bad faith in a gutter in outer space,
prosthetic eyes and prefrontal cortex
orbit around Earth, an "I" (circa
20th Century) in the sky watching.

The SUV with DDTs, retrorockets,
and artificial gravity bee-line
to reptilian trajectory at every scare
by planet three sociopaths.

A dream dog with heels and opposable thumbs,
the domesticated animal cloaks
gladiators thrilled by goal posts and tailgates.

Space station reflection mirrors
for deliberation on greenhouse gases
by the two-faced Homo sapiens from the Oz-zone
where self-consciousness gilds every deed.

With trophy cases filled and stacked,
poor sports alone expect to receive apologies
while rested envy and resentment rise
from the bench and enter the coliseum.

Space Cadet

At the human zoo words build the cages
from which eyes and mouths
observe, question, and emote superiority.

The de-fanged beast on two legs
grumbles or smiles over the food,
providing information to the keeper crew:
psychologist, sociologist, economist, novelist.

Pacing back and forth, if the animal
wasn't crazy when captured,
when confined, mad describes paws
and sudden lunges to the left and to the right.

Once convinced a god jimmied at the lock
enough to free energy enough for imitation,
with limitation, a jester courted disaster:
empire, genetic tricks, electrocuted gestures.

With the chance found in mines
for lightheartedness the pointed-headed geek
left behind the wrung chicken necks to squat in cells
on a pad without serif or seraph for launch.

Bubble Bath

The film studies student in every community
pokes around the soapy substance and discovers.
Hysterics bursts open to bubble world
where prescription lenses occupy eyeball sockets:
O me, O my, a not wholly one bathes in perspectives.

Each bead from the foam froth communes
in view point habits and rituals, a magic
adhesive for the droplet circle separation.
Should seepage leak from glob to glob,
all hell savages ravage in efforts to form a globe.

Within a single air sac for pupils cornea
background props prop-up "initiatives"
with "outside-the-box" blather
for the blind-spotted mope not failing better
or learning during the deflation.

In a dark room with lather all around
the world history con pop lover navigates
without a concession stand to find
the Homo sapiens secret.

Space Travel

Becoming until dust and orbiting gas,
despite stock role calls from mob directors,
the foot-print designer records for dancers,
choreographers, and the steadfast:
Here, here and.

For the syllable hoofer,
the sidewalk and office audiences
focus on the faint tint coming and going
from supporting actor dressing room
or leading man suite:
Experience escapes as routine
from the unique momentary engagement.

Molds and templates cliché
and stamp without character:
redundant over-crowds.

Calling out to the empty "I am"
from behind the dido smile,
the mutating sole marker halts on every word
to wait on specific answers at a line break.

Space Craft Obit

Driving the vehicle across a lifetime,
each pit-stop crew member takes to the wheel.

The poem peers out through hawk pupils
prepared to learn insight, inscape,
perspective that could change history, tomorrow.

Sitting in a cockpit on a metaphor,
adjustable to irony at the larynx,
the cabby floors the pedal for take-off.

The keys jingle as the grip on the shift stick
and Brodie knob makes for the medallion.

Verb for verb and mind for mind,
a daredevil engages at light speed
along and among line enjambments.

Without streets or map, without trajectory,
each test pilot in the habit capsule,
the habitat contraption, traverses
the symbolic order horizon
where ideology thins for possibility: Space craft.

Every vague notion emerges for retrieval
to where few nervous pacers recognize a word.

9 781666 706109